Easy Learning JDBC+MySQL

YANG HU

The complexity of life, because they do not understand to simplify the complex, simple is the beginning of wisdom. From the essence of practice, this book to briefly explain the concept and vividly cultivate programming interest.

http://en.verejava.com

ISBN: 9781095114735

CONTENTS

JDBC connect MySQL CURD

If you need to learn MySQL basics, please read my book
<<Easy Learning MySQL SQL>>

http://en.verejava.com

1. Download jdbc to connect mysql driver jar
   mysql-connector-java-5.1.45-bin.jar

   http://en.verejava.com/download.jsp?id=1

2. Open cmd console and login to MySQL with your username/password and then create a database : test

---

Mysql –uroot –p19810109

create database test**;**

---

3. Open database test and then create a table: users

```
uses test;

create table users
(
    id int primary key auto_increment,
    username varchar(100),
    pwd varchar(100)
);
```

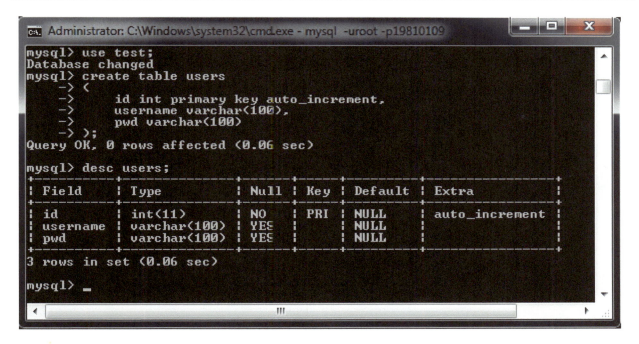

4. Open Eclipse and create a java project test

Add mysql-connector-java-5.1.45-bin.jar to test java project

5. Add TestAdd.java to insert data to users table

```java
import java.sql.*;
public class TestAdd {
    public static void main(String[] args) {
        Connection conn = null;
        try {
            // Load MySQL driver by mysql-connector-java-3.0.10-stable-bin.jar
            Class.forName("com.mysql.jdbc.Driver");

            //Create connection
            // ip : 192.168.1.104  database name : test , username : root , password : 19810109
            conn =
DriverManager.getConnection("jdbc:mysql://192.168.1.104/test?useUnicode=true&amp;
characterEncoding=utf-8", "root", "19810109");

            //sql statement insert data to table: users
            String sql = "insert into users(username,pwd)values('David','111111')";
            Statement stmt = conn.createStatement();
            stmt.executeUpdate(sql);  //executes the sql
        } catch (Exception e) {
            e.printStackTrace();
        } finally {
            try {
                conn.close();
            } catch (SQLException e) {
                e.printStackTrace();
            }
        }
    }
}
```

Result:

5

6. Add TestFind.java Read data from users table

```java
import java.sql.*;
public class TestFind {
    public static void main(String[] args) {
        Connection conn = null;
        try {
            Class.forName("com.mysql.jdbc.Driver");
            conn =
DriverManager.getConnection("jdbc:mysql://192.168.1.104/test?useUnicode=true&amp;
characterEncoding=utf-8", "root", "19810109");

            String sql = "select * from users"; // get all data from table: users

            Statement stmt = conn.createStatement();
            ResultSet rs = stmt.executeQuery(sql); //return all users into ResultSet

            while (rs.next()) {
                int id = rs.getInt("id");
                String username = rs.getString("username");
                String pwd = rs.getString("pwd");
                System.out.println(id + "," + username + "," + pwd);
            }
        } catch (Exception e) {
            e.printStackTrace();
        } finally {
            try {
                conn.close();
            } catch (SQLException e) {
                e.printStackTrace();
            }
        }
    }
}
```

Result:

Problems @ Javadoc Declaration Console

`<terminated>` TestFind [Java Application] C:\Program Files (x86)\Java

```
1,David,111111
```

6

7. Add TestUpdate.java Update data to users table

```java
import java.sql.*;
public class TestUpdate {
    public static void main(String[] args) {
        Connection conn = null;
        try {
            Class.forName("com.mysql.jdbc.Driver");
            conn =
DriverManager.getConnection("jdbc:mysql://192.168.1.104/test?useUnicode=true&amp;amp;
characterEncoding=utf-8", "root", "19810109");

            //sql statement update data to table: users
            String sql = "update users set pwd='222222' where id=1";

            Statement stmt = conn.createStatement();
            stmt.executeUpdate(sql);
        } catch (Exception e) {
            e.printStackTrace();
        } finally {
            try {
                conn.close();
            } catch (SQLException e) {
                e.printStackTrace();
            }
        }
    }
}
```

Result:

8. Add TestDelete.java delete data from users table

```java
import java.sql.*;
public class TestDelete {
    public static void main(String[] args) {
        Connection conn = null;
        try {
            Class.forName("com.mysql.jdbc.Driver");
            conn =
DriverManager.getConnection("jdbc:mysql://192.168.1.104/test?useUnicode=true&amp;amp;
characterEncoding=utf-8", "root", "19810109");

            //sql statement delete data from table: users
            String sql = "delete from users where id=1";

            Statement stmt = conn.createStatement();
            stmt.executeUpdate(sql);
        } catch (Exception e) {
            e.printStackTrace();
        } finally {
            try {
                conn.close();
            } catch (SQLException e) {
                e.printStackTrace();
            }
        }
    }
}
```

Result:

8

JDBC Precompiled CRUD

JDBC pre-compile mode is faster, because it will pre-compile sql into cache

1. Create a table : book in test database

```sql
create table book
(
    id int primary key auto_increment,
    title varchar(100),
    price decimal(10,2),
    birth timestamp,
    publish_date timestamp,
    update_date timestamp
);
```

Result:

```
mysql>
mysql> create table book
    -> (
    ->      id int primary key auto_increment,
    ->      title varchar(100),
    ->      price decimal(10,2),
    ->      birth timestamp,
    ->      publish_date timestamp,
    ->      update_date timestamp
    -> );
Query OK, 0 rows affected (0.03 sec)

mysql>
mysql> desc book
    -> ;
+--------------+---------------+------+-----+---------------------+-------+
| Field        | Type          | Null | Key | Default             | Extra |
+--------------+---------------+------+-----+---------------------+-------+
| id           | int(11)       | NO   | PRI | NULL                | auto_in
nt |
| title        | varchar(100)  | YES  |     | NULL                |       |
| price        | decimal(10,2) | YES  |     | NULL                |       |
| birth        | timestamp     | YES  |     | CURRENT_TIMESTAMP   |       |
| publish_date | timestamp     | YES  |     | 0000-00-00 00:00:00 |       |
| update_date  | timestamp     | YES  |     | 0000-00-00 00:00:00 |       |
+--------------+---------------+------+-----+---------------------+-------+
6 rows in set (0.06 sec)

mysql> _
```

2. Precompilation mode Add book record

```java
import java.sql.*;
public class TestAdd {
  public static void main(String[] args) {
    Connection conn = null;
    try {
      Class.forName("com.mysql.jdbc.Driver");
      conn =
DriverManager.getConnection("jdbc:mysql://192.168.1.104/test?useUnicode=true&characterEncoding=utf-8", "root", "19810109");

      //Precompilation mode insert data to table: book
      String sql = "insert into
book(title,price,birth,publish_date,update_date)values(?,?,?,?,?)";

      PreparedStatement pstmt = conn.prepareStatement(sql);
      pstmt.setString(1, "Easy Learning Java");
      pstmt.setFloat(2, 40.55f);
      pstmt.setTimestamp(3, new Timestamp(new Date().getTime()));
      pstmt.setTimestamp(4, new Timestamp(new Date().getTime()));
      pstmt.setTimestamp(5, new Timestamp(new Date().getTime()));
      pstmt.executeUpdate();//executes the sql
    } catch (Exception e) {
      e.printStackTrace();
    } finally {
      try {
        conn.close();
      } catch (SQLException e) {
        e.printStackTrace();
      }
    }
  }
}
```

Result:

11

3. Precompilation mode Find the data of the book by record id=1

```java
import java.sql.*;
public class TestFind {
   public static void main(String[] args) {
      Connection conn = null;
      try {
         Class.forName("com.mysql.jdbc.Driver");
         conn =
DriverManager.getConnection("jdbc:mysql://192.168.1.104/test?useUnicode=true&characterEncoding=utf-8", "root", "19810109");

         //Precompilation mode sql statement query data from book
         String sql = "select * from book where id=?";

         PreparedStatement pstmt = conn.prepareStatement(sql);
         pstmt.setInt(1, 1);

         ResultSet rs = pstmt.executeQuery();
         while (rs.next()) {
            int id = rs.getInt("id");
            String title = rs.getString("title");
            float price = rs.getFloat("price");
            String birth = rs.getString("birth");
            Timestamp publish_date = rs.getTimestamp("publish_date");
            Timestamp update_date = rs.getTimestamp("update_date");
            System.out.println(id + "," + title + "," + price + "," + birth + "," + publish_date + ","
+ update_date);
         }
      } catch (Exception e) {
         e.printStackTrace();
      } finally {
         try {
            conn.close();
         } catch (SQLException e) {
            e.printStackTrace();
         }
      }
   }
}
```

Result:
1,Easy Learning Java,40.55,2019-04-17 16:09:34,2019-04-17 16:09:35.0,2019-04-17 16:09:35.0

4. Precompilation mode Modify the book record id=1

```java
import java.sql.*;
import java.util.Date;

public class TestUpdate {

    public static void main(String[] args) {
        Connection conn = null;
        try {
            Class.forName("com.mysql.jdbc.Driver");
            conn =
DriverManager.getConnection("jdbc:mysql://192.168.1.104/test?useUnicode=true&characterE
ncoding=utf-8", "root", "19810109");

            //Precompilation mode update data into book
            String sql = "update book set title=?,price=?,birth=?,publish_date=?,update_date=?
where id=?";
            PreparedStatement pstmt = conn.prepareStatement(sql);
            pstmt.setString(1, "Life is not limited");
            pstmt.setFloat(2, 50.55f);
            pstmt.setDate(3, new java.sql.Date(new Date().getTime()));
            pstmt.setTimestamp(4, new Timestamp(new Date().getTime()));
            pstmt.setTimestamp(5, new Timestamp(new Date().getTime()));
            pstmt.setInt(6, 1);

            pstmt.executeUpdate();//executes the sql

        } catch (Exception e) {
            e.printStackTrace();
        } finally {
            try {
                conn.close();
            } catch (SQLException e) {
                e.printStackTrace();
            }
        }
    }
}
```

Result:

```
mysql> select * from book;
+----+-------------------+-------+---------------------+---------------------+
| id | title             | price | birth               | publish_date        |
| update_date                                |
+----+-------------------+-------+---------------------+---------------------+
|  1 | Life is not limited | 50.55 | 2019-04-17 00:00:00 | 2019-04-17 16:22:15 |
| 2019-04-17 16:22:15 |
+----+-------------------+-------+---------------------+---------------------+
1 row in set (0.00 sec)

mysql>
```

5. Precompilation mode Delete the book by record id=1

```java
import java.sql.*;
import java.util.Date;
public class TestDelete {
    public static void main(String[] args) {
        Connection conn = null;
        try {
            Class.forName("com.mysql.jdbc.Driver");
            conn =
DriverManager.getConnection("jdbc:mysql://192.168.1.104/test?useUnicode=true&characterEncoding=utf-8", "root", "19810109");

            //Precompilation mode sql statement delete data from book
            String sql = "delete from book where id=?";
            PreparedStatement pstmt = conn.prepareStatement(sql);
            pstmt.setInt(1, 1);

            pstmt.executeUpdate();
        } catch (Exception e) {
            e.printStackTrace();
        } finally {
            try {
                conn.close();
            } catch (SQLException e) {
                e.printStackTrace();
            }
        }
    }
}
```

Result:

JDBC Tool DBUtil

```
                        DBUtil
─────────────────────────────────────────
◆DBUtil()
◆openConnection() : Connection
◆executeUpdate(sql : String) : boolean
◆executeQuery(sql : String) : ResultSet
◆executeUpdate(sql : String, params : Object[]) : boolean
◆executeQuery(sql : String, params : Object[]) : ResultSet
◆DBClose()
```

```java
import java.sql.*;
import java.util.Date;

public class DBUtil {

    protected Connection conn;
    protected Statement stmt;

    public DBUtil() {
        try {
            Class.forName("com.mysql.jdbc.Driver");
        } catch (ClassNotFoundException e) {
            e.printStackTrace();
        }
    }

    //Open JDBC Database Connection
    public Connection openConnection() {
        try {
            return DriverManager.getConnection("jdbc:mysql://
192.168.1.104/test?useUnicode=true&characterEncoding=utf-8", "root", "19810109");
        } catch (SQLException e) {
            e.printStackTrace();
        }
        return null;
    }
```

```java
//execute add delete update sql
public boolean executeUpdate(String sql) {
    conn = openConnection();

    try {
        Statement stmt = conn.createStatement();
        if (stmt.executeUpdate(sql) > 0) {
            return true;
        }
    } catch (SQLException e) {
        e.printStackTrace();
    } finally {
        if (conn != null) {
            try {
                conn.close();
            } catch (SQLException e) {
                e.printStackTrace();
            }
        }
    }
    return false;
}

//execute query sql
public ResultSet executeQuery(String sql) {
    conn = openConnection();
    try {
        Statement stmt = conn.createStatement();
        return stmt.executeQuery(sql);
    } catch (SQLException e) {
        e.printStackTrace();
    }
    return null;
}
```

```java
//Precompilation Add Delete Update
public boolean executeUpdate(String sql, Object[] params) {
    conn = openConnection();
    try {
        PreparedStatement pstmt = conn.prepareStatement(sql);
        for (int i = 0; params != null && i < params.length; i++) {
            Object param = params[i];
            if (param instanceof Integer) {
                pstmt.setInt(i + 1, Integer.parseInt(param.toString()));
            }
            if (param instanceof Float) {
                pstmt.setFloat(i + 1, Float.parseFloat(param.toString()));
            }
            if (param instanceof Double) {
                pstmt.setDouble(i + 1, Double.parseDouble(param.toString()));
            }
            if (param instanceof String) {
                pstmt.setString(i + 1, param.toString());
            }
            if (param instanceof Date) {
                java.util.Date date = (java.util.Date) param;
                pstmt.setTimestamp(i + 1, new Timestamp(date.getTime()));
            }
        }
        if (pstmt.executeUpdate() > 0) {
            return true;
        }
    } catch (SQLException e) {
        e.printStackTrace();
    } finally {
        DBClose();
    }
    return false;
}
```

```java
//select * from book where id=? and title=?;
public ResultSet executeQuery(String sql, Object[] params) {
    conn = openConnection();
    try {
        PreparedStatement pstmt = conn.prepareStatement(sql);
        for (int i = 0; params != null && i < params.length; i++) {
            Object param = params[i];
            if (param instanceof Integer) {
                pstmt.setInt(i + 1, Integer.parseInt(param.toString()));
            }
            if (param instanceof Float) {
                pstmt.setFloat(i + 1, Float.parseFloat(param.toString()));
            }
            if (param instanceof Double) {
                pstmt.setDouble(i + 1, Double.parseDouble(param.toString()));
            }
            if (param instanceof String) {
                pstmt.setString(i + 1, param.toString());
            }
            if (param instanceof Date) {
                java.util.Date date = (java.util.Date) param;
                pstmt.setTimestamp(i + 1, new Timestamp(date.getTime()));
            }
        }
        return pstmt.executeQuery();
    } catch (SQLException e) {
        e.printStackTrace();
    }
    return null;
}

public void DBClose() {
    if (conn != null) {
        try {
            conn.close();
        } catch (SQLException e) {
            e.printStackTrace();
        }
    }
}
}
```

DBUtil User CRUD

1. Create a model class: User mapping table : users

```java
public class User {
    private int id;
    private String username;
    private String pwd;

    public User() {

    }

    public User(String username, String pwd) {
        super();
        this.username = username;
        this.pwd = pwd;
    }

    public User(int id, String username, String pwd) {
        super();
        this.id = id;
        this.username = username;
        this.pwd = pwd;
    }

    public int getId() {
        return id;
    }

    public void setId(int id) {
        this.id = id;
    }
```

```java
    public String getUsername() {
        return username;
    }

    public void setUsername(String username) {
        this.username = username;
    }

    public String getPwd() {
        return pwd;
    }

    public void setPwd(String pwd) {
        this.pwd = pwd;
    }

}
```

2. DBUtil adds the User to the users table

```java
public class TestAdd {

    public static void main(String[] args) {
        DBUtil db = new DBUtil();

        User user = new User();
        user.setUsername("Grace");
        user.setPwd("444444");

        String sql = "insert into users(username,pwd)values('" + user.getUsername() + "','" +
user.getPwd() + "')";
        db.executeUpdate(sql);
    }
}
```

Result:

3. DBUtil reads the data of the users table with id=2 and stores it in the User.

```java
import java.sql.*;
public class TestFindOne {

    public static void main(String[] args) {
        DBUtil db = new DBUtil();
        String sql = "select * from users where id=2 ";
        ResultSet rs = db.executeQuery(sql);

        User user = null;
        try {
            if (rs.next()) {
                user = new User();
                user.setId(rs.getInt("id"));
                user.setUsername(rs.getString("username"));
                user.setPwd(rs.getString("pwd"));
            }
        } catch (SQLException e) {
            e.printStackTrace();
        } finally {
            db.DBClose();
        }

        if (user != null) {
            System.out.println(user.getId() + "," + user.getUsername() + "," + user.getPwd());
        }
    }
}
```

Result:

Problems @ Javadoc Declaration Console

<terminated> TestFindOne [Java Application] C:\Program Files (x86)\

```
2,Grace,444444
```

4. DBUtil update the data of the users table id=2

```java
public class TestUpdate {

    public static void main(String[] args) {
        DBUtil db = new DBUtil();

        User user = new User();
        user.setId(2);

        String sql = "update users set pwd='555555' where id=" + user.getId();
        db.executeUpdate(sql);
    }
}
```

Result:

5. DBUtil deletes the data of the users table id=2

```java
public class TestDelete {

  public static void main(String[] args) {
    DBUtil db = new DBUtil();

    User user = new User();
    user.setId(2);

    String sql = "delete from users where id=" + user.getId();
    db.executeUpdate(sql);
  }
}
```

Result:

```
Administrator: C:\Windows\system32\cmd.exe - mysql  -uroot -p19810109

mysql> select * from users;
Empty set (0.00 sec)

mysql>
```

6. DBUtil reads multiple data of users and stores it in List<User>

Insert 2 items data into table : users;

---

insert into users(username,pwd)values('James','666666');

insert into users(username,pwd)values('Isacc','777777');

Create TestFind.java

```java
import java.sql.*;
import java.util.*;
public class TestFind {
    public static void main(String[] args) {
        DBUtil db = new DBUtil();
        String sql = "select * from users";
        ResultSet rs = db.executeQuery(sql);

        List<User> userList = new ArrayList<User>();
        try {
            while (rs.next()) {
                User user = new User();
                user.setId(rs.getInt("id"));
                user.setUsername(rs.getString("username"));
                user.setPwd(rs.getString("pwd"));
                userList.add(user);
            }
        } catch (SQLException e) {
            e.printStackTrace();
        } finally {
            db.DBClose();
        }

        for (int i = 0; i < userList.size(); i++) {
            User user = userList.get(i);
            System.out.println(user.getId() + "," + user.getUsername() + "," + user.getPwd());
        }
    }
}
```

Result:

Problems @ Javadoc Declaration Console ⊠

\<terminated\> TestFind (2) [Java Application] C:\Program Files (x86)\J

```
3,James,666666
4,Isacc,777777
```

DBUtil UserDAO CRUD

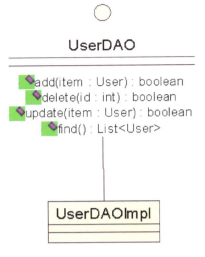

1. Create a data access interface: UserDAO

```java
import java.util.*;

public interface UserDAO {

    public boolean add(User item);

    public boolean delete(int id);

    public boolean update(User item);

    public List<User> find();
}
```

2. Data access implementation class : UserDAOImpl

```java
import java.sql.*;
import java.util.*;

public class UserDAOImpl implements UserDAO {

  private DBUtil db;

  public UserDAOImpl() {
    db = new DBUtil();
  }

  @Override
  public boolean add(User item) {
    String sql = "insert into users(username,pwd)values(?,?)";
    Object[] params={item.getUsername(),item.getPwd()};

    return db.executeUpdate(sql, params);
  }

  @Override
  public boolean delete(int id) {
    String sql = "delete from users where id=" + id;
    return db.executeUpdate(sql);
  }

  @Override
  public boolean update(User item) {
    String sql = "update users set username=?,pwd=? where id =?" ;
    Object[] params={item.getUsername(),item.getPwd(),item.getId()};

    return db.executeUpdate(sql, params);
  }
```

```java
@Override
public List<User> find() {
    List<User> userList = new ArrayList<User>();
    String sql = "select * from users";
    ResultSet rs = db.executeQuery(sql);
    try {
        while (rs.next()) {
            int id = rs.getInt("id");
            String username = rs.getString("username");
            String pwd = rs.getString("pwd");
            userList.add(new User(id, username, pwd));
        }
    } catch (SQLException e) {
        e.printStackTrace();
    } finally {
        db.DBClose();
    }
    return userList;
}

}
```

3. UserDAO TestAdd

```java
public class TestAdd {

    public static void main(String[] args) {

        UserDAO userDAO = new UserDAOImpl();
        userDAO.add(new User("Sala", '888888'));

    }
}
```

Result:

```
mysql> select * from users;
+----+----------+--------+
| id | username | pwd    |
+----+----------+--------+
|  3 | James    | 666666 |
|  4 | Isacc    | 777777 |
|  5 | Sala     | 888888 |
+----+----------+--------+
3 rows in set (0.00 sec)

mysql>
```

4. UserDAO TestFind

```java
import java.util.*;
public class TestFind {

    public static void main(String[] args) {

        UserDAO userDAO = new UserDAOImpl();
        List<User> userList = userDAO.find();

        for (User item : userList) {
            System.out.println(item.getId() + "," + item.getUsername() + "," + item.getPwd());
        }

    }
}
```

Result:

```
Problems  @ Javadoc  Declaration  Console ☒

<terminated> TestFind (3) [Java Application] C:\Program Files (x86)\J
3,James,666666
4,Isacc,777777
5,Sala,888888
```

5. UserDAO TestUpdate

```java
public class TestUpdate {

    public static void main(String[] args) {

        UserDAO userDAO = new UserDAOImpl();
        userDAO.update(new User(5, "Sala", "999999"));

    }
}
```

Result:

33

6. UserDAO TestDelete

```java
public class TestDelete {

  public static void main(String[] args) {

    UserDAO userDAO = new UserDAOImpl();
    userDAO.delete(5);

  }
}
```

Result:

DBUtil UserDAO Paging Query

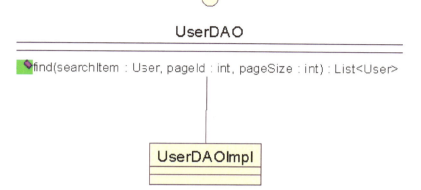

UserDAO

find(searchItem : User, pageId : int, pageSize : int) : List<User>

UserDAOImpl

1. Create a data access interface: UserDAO

```
import java.util.*;

public interface UserDAO {

    public List<User> find(User searchItem,int pageId,int pageSize);

}
```

2. Data access implementation class : UserDAOImpl

```java
import java.sql.*;
import java.util.*;
public class UserDAOImpl implements UserDAO {
    private DBUtil db;

    public UserDAOImpl() {
        db = new DBUtil();
    }

    public List<User> find(User searchItem, int pageId, int pageSize) {
        ResultSet rs = null;
        List<User> userList = new ArrayList<User>();
        try {
            boolean b = false;
            StringBuffer where = new StringBuffer();
            String fvalue = null;
            fvalue = searchItem.getUsername();
            if (fvalue != null && fvalue.length() > 0) {
                if (b)
                    where.append(" and");
                where.append(" username like '%" + fvalue + "%'");
                b = true;
            }
            if (!where.toString().equals(""))
                where.insert(0, " where ");

            String sql = "select * from  users  " + where.toString() + " order by id asc limit " +
(pageId - 1) * pageSize + "," + pageSize;
            rs = db.executeQuery(sql);
            while (rs.next()) {
                int id = rs.getInt("id");
                String username = rs.getString("username");
                String pwd = rs.getString("pwd");
                userList.add(new User(id, username, pwd));
            }
        } catch (SQLException e) {
            e.printStackTrace();
        } finally {
            db.DBClose();
        }
        return userList;
    }
}
```

3. Insert test data into table : users

insert into users(username,pwd)**values**('David','111111')**;**
insert into users(username,pwd)**values**('Sala','222222')**;**
insert into users(username,pwd)**values**('Mathew','333333')**;**
insert into users(username,pwd)**values**('Luka','4444444')**;**
insert into users(username,pwd)**values**('John','555555')**;**

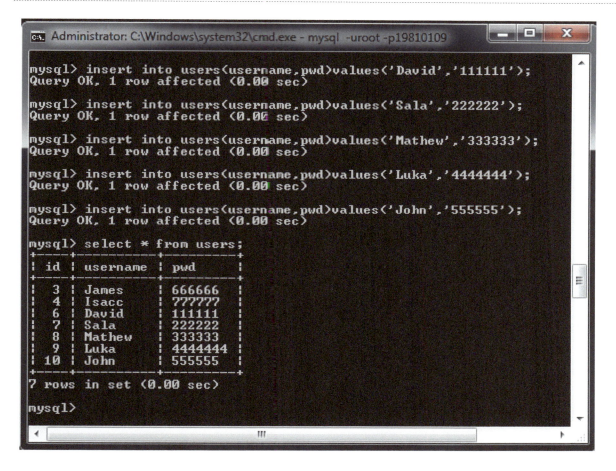

4. Get the first page data from : users

```java
import java.text.SimpleDateFormat;
import java.util.*;
public class TestFind {

    public static void main(String[] args) {

        int pageId = 1; //Current page
        int pageSize = 3; //Number of records per page
        User searchItem = new User();
        searchItem.setUsername("");

        UserDAO userDAO = new UserDAOImpl();
        List<User> userList = userDAO.find(searchItem, pageId, pageSize);
        for (User item : userList) {
            System.out.println(item.getId() + "," + item. getUsername() + "," + item.getPwd());
        }
    }
}
```

Result:

```
Problems  @ Javadoc  Declaration  Console
3,James,666666
4,Isacc,777777
6,David,111111
```

5. change int pageId = 2; Get the second page data from : users

```
Problems  @ Javadoc  Declaration  Console
7,Sala,222222
8,Mathew,333333
9,Luka,4444444
```

JDBC Reflections Any Object

1. Create a class: Session Save any Object by reflection

```java
import java.lang.reflect.*;
import java.util.*;

public class Session {
  private DBUtil db;

  public Session() {
    db = new DBUtil();
  }

  public boolean save(Object obj,String tableName) {
    Class clazz = obj.getClass();
    String className = clazz.getName(); //Get the full class name

    try {
      clazz = Class.forName(className);

      //Get the properties of any model class as the column name of the table
      Field[] fields = clazz.getDeclaredFields();

      //Get the built insert sql statement
      Object[] returnObj = buildInsertSQL(fields, obj, tableName);
      String sql = returnObj[0].toString();
      Object[] params = (Object[]) returnObj[1];

      return db.executeUpdate(sql, params);
    } catch (Exception e) {
      e.printStackTrace();
    } finally {
      db.DBClose();
    }
    return false;
  }
```

```java
private Object[] buildInsertSQL(Field[] fields, Object obj, String tableName) {
    Object[] returnObj = new Object[2];
    Class clazz = obj.getClass();

    List<Object> params = new ArrayList<Object>();
    StringBuffer sb = new StringBuffer();
    StringBuffer sbValue = new StringBuffer();

    sb.append("insert into ").append(tableName).append("(");
    for (int i = 0; i < fields.length; i++) {
        Field field = fields[i];
        String fieldName = field.getName();

        if ("id".equals(fieldName)) {
            continue;
        }

        sb.append(fieldName).append(",");
        sbValue.append("?,");

        String firstFieldName = fieldName.substring(0, 1).toUpperCase();
        String leftFieldName = fieldName.substring(1);
        String methodName = "get" + firstFieldName + leftFieldName;

        Method method;
        try {
            method = clazz.getDeclaredMethod(methodName, new Class[] {});
            Object resultObj = method.invoke(obj, new Object[] {});
            params.add(resultObj);
        } catch (Exception e) {
            e.printStackTrace();
        }
    }
    sb.delete(sb.length() - 1, sb.length());
    sb.append(")values(");
    sbValue.delete(sbValue.length() - 1, sbValue.length());
    sb.append(sbValue).append(")");
    returnObj[0] = sb.toString();
    returnObj[1] = params.toArray();
    return returnObj;
}
}
```

2. Create Testing class: TestSessionAdd.java

```java
public class TestSessionAdd {

  public static void main(String[] args) {

    Session session=new Session();

    User user=new User("Ablahan","888888");
    session.save(user,"users");

    User user2=new User("Make","999999");
    session.save(user2,"users");

    User user3=new User("Lebeka","101010");
    session.save(user3,"users");

  }
}
```

Result:

JDBC Transaction

Transaction: All SQL commits successfully, or all rollback fails

1. 10 data inserted in bulk

```java
import java.sql.*;
import java.util.Date;
public class TestTransaction {
    public static void main(String[] args) {
        DBUtil db = new DBUtil();
        Connection conn = db.openConnection();
        try {
            conn.setAutoCommit(false);//Set to manually submit
            for (int i = 0; i < 10; i++) {
                String sql = "insert into book(title,price,birth,publish_date,update_date)values(?,?,?,?,?)";

                PreparedStatement pstmt = conn.prepareStatement(sql);
                pstmt.setString(1, "Motivating books " + i);
                pstmt.setFloat(2, 40.55f + 1);
                pstmt.setTimestamp(3, new Timestamp(new Date().getTime()));
                pstmt.setTimestamp(4, new Timestamp(new Date().getTime()));
                pstmt.setTimestamp(5, new Timestamp(new Date().getTime()));

                pstmt.executeUpdate();
                conn.commit();// 10 data inserted, batch submit
            }
        } catch (SQLException e) {
            try {
                //10 pieces of data rollback Insertion failed
                conn.rollback();
            } catch (SQLException e1) {
                e1.printStackTrace();
            }
            e.printStackTrace();
        } finally {
            db.DBClose();
        }
    }
}
```

Result:

```
mysql> select * from book;
+------+--------------------+--------+---------------------+--------------
----------------------+
| id  | title              | price  | birth               | publish_da
update_date         |
+------+--------------------+--------+---------------------+--------------
----------------------+
|  2  | Motivating books 0 | 41.55  | 2019-04-18 10:19:15 | 2019-04-18
2019-04-18 10:19:16 |
|  3  | Motivating books 1 | 41.55  | 2019-04-18 10:19:16 | 2019-04-18
2019-04-18 10:19:16 |
|  4  | Motivating books 2 | 41.55  | 2019-04-18 10:19:16 | 2019-04-18
2019-04-18 10:19:16 |
|  5  | Motivating books 3 | 41.55  | 2019-04-18 10:19:16 | 2019-04-18
2019-04-18 10:19:16 |
|  6  | Motivating books 4 | 41.55  | 2019-04-18 10:19:16 | 2019-04-18
2019-04-18 10:19:16 |
|  7  | Motivating books 5 | 41.55  | 2019-04-18 10:19:16 | 2019-04-18
2019-04-18 10:19:16 |
|  8  | Motivating books 6 | 41.55  | 2019-04-18 10:19:16 | 2019-04-18
2019-04-18 10:19:16 |
|  9  | Motivating books 7 | 41.55  | 2019-04-18 10:19:16 | 2019-04-18
2019-04-18 10:19:16 |
| 10  | Motivating books 8 | 41.55  | 2019-04-18 10:19:16 | 2019-04-18
2019-04-18 10:19:16 |
| 11  | Motivating books 9 | 41.55  | 2019-04-18 10:19:16 | 2019-04-18
2019-04-18 10:19:16 |
+------+--------------------+--------+---------------------+--------------
----------------------+
10 rows in set (0.00 sec)
```

43

JDBC Save and Export Text File

1. Create a table: textfile to store a text file

```
create table textfile
(
    id int primary key auto_increment,
    content longtext
);
```

```
Administrator: C:\Windows\system32\cmd.exe - mysql  -uroot -p19810109

mysql> create table textfile
    -> (
    ->        id int primary key auto_increment,
    ->        content longtext
    -> );
Query OK, 0 rows affected (0.02 sec)

mysql> desc textfile;
+---------+----------+------+-----+---------+----------------+
| Field   | Type     | Null | Key | Default | Extra          |
+---------+----------+------+-----+---------+----------------+
| id      | int(11)  | NO   | PRI | NULL    | auto_increment |
| content | longtext | YES  |     | NULL    |                |
+---------+----------+------+-----+---------+----------------+
2 rows in set (0.02 sec)

mysql>
```

2. Create a text file: text.txt content below

Having a specific meaning and purpose in your life helps to encourage you towards living a fulfilling and inspired life.

My friends, love is better than anger. Hope is better than fear. Optimism is better than despair. So let us be loving, hopeful and optimistic. And we'll change the world.

3. Save the text.txt to the content field of the table: textfile

```java
import java.io.*;
import java.sql.*;

public class TestAdd {

    public static void main(String[] args) {

        DBUtil db = new DBUtil();
        Connection conn = db.openConnection();
        String sql = "insert into textfile(content)values(?)";

        try {
            PreparedStatement pstmt = conn.prepareStatement(sql);
            File file = new File("C:/Users/tim/Desktop/text.txt");
            Reader reader = new FileReader(file);
            pstmt.setCharacterStream(1, reader, (int)file.length());
            pstmt.executeUpdate();

        } catch (Exception e) {
            e.printStackTrace();
        } finally {
            db.DBClose();
        }
    }
}
```

Result:

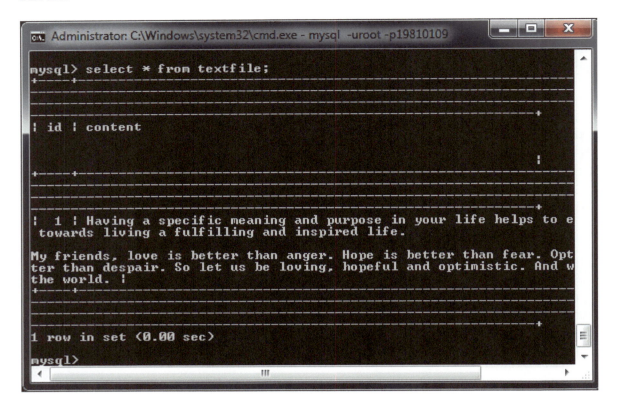

4. Read content field of the table: textfile to store in text2.txt

```java
import java.io.*;
import java.sql.*;
public class TestFind {

    public static void main(String[] args) {
        DBUtil db = new DBUtil();
        Connection conn = db.openConnection();
        String sql = "select * from textfile where id=1";

        try {
            PreparedStatement pstmt = conn.prepareStatement(sql);
            ResultSet rs = pstmt.executeQuery(sql);

            StringBuilder sb = new StringBuilder();
            if (rs.next()) {
                Reader reader = rs.getCharacterStream("content");
                int l = 0;
                char[] cbuf = new char[1024];
                while ((l = reader.read(cbuf)) != -1) {
                    sb.append(new String(cbuf, 0, l));
                }
            }

            //Save the read data to test2.txt
            Writer writer = new FileWriter(new File("C:/Users/tim/Desktop/test2.txt"));
            writer.write(sb.toString());
            writer.flush();
            writer.close();
        } catch (Exception e) {
            e.printStackTrace();
        } finally {
            db.DBClose();
        }
    }
}
```

Result:

test2.txt

Having a specific meaning and purpose in your life helps to encourage you towards living a fulfilling and inspired life.

My friends, love is better than anger. Hope is better than fear. Optimism is better than despair. So let us be loving, hopeful and optimistic. And we'll change the world.

JDBC Save and Export Picture

1. Create a table: binaryfile to store a picture

```
create table binaryfile
(
    id int primary key auto_increment,
    file mediumblob
);
```

2. Save the java.jpg to the file field of the table: binaryfile

```java
import java.io.*;
import java.sql.*;

public class TestAdd {

    public static void main(String[] args) {

        DBUtil db = new DBUtil();
        Connection conn = db.openConnection();
        String sql = "insert into binaryfile(file)values(?)";

        try {
            PreparedStatement pstmt = conn.prepareStatement(sql);
            File file = new File("C:/Users/tim/Desktop/java.jpg");
            InputStream inputStream = new FileInputStream(file);
            pstmt.setBlob(1, inputStream, (int)file.length());
            pstmt.executeUpdate();
        } catch (Exception e) {
            e.printStackTrace();
        } finally {
            db.DBClose();
        }

    }
}
```

4. Read file field of the table: binaryfile to store in java2.jpg

```java
import java.io.*;
import java.sql.*;

public class TestFind {

  public static void main(String[] args) {
    DBUtil db = new DBUtil();
    Connection conn = db.openConnection();
    String sql = "select * from binaryfile where id=1";

    OutputStream os = null;
    try {
      PreparedStatement pstmt = conn.prepareStatement(sql);
      ResultSet rs = pstmt.executeQuery();
      os = new FileOutputStream("C:/Users/tim/Desktop/java2.jpg");
      while (rs.next()) {
        Blob blob = rs.getBlob("file");
        InputStream is = blob.getBinaryStream();
        int l = 0;
        byte[] data = new byte[1024];
        while ((l = is.read(data)) != -1) {
          os.write(data, 0, l);
        }
        os.flush();
      }
    } catch (Exception e) {
      e.printStackTrace();
    } finally {
      try {
        os.close();
      } catch (IOException e) {
        e.printStackTrace();
      }
      db.DBClose();
    }
  }
}
```

Result:

java2.jpg

Easy Learning

Java

Beginners to learn Java better fast (3 Edition)

JDBC Call Stored Procedure Add User

1. Create a stored procedure: sp_user_add in MySQL

```
DELIMITER $
create procedure sp_user_add(in ir_username varchar(20),in in_pwd varchar(20))
begin
  insert into users(username,pwd)values(in_username,in_pwd);
end $
```

```
mysql> DELIMITER $
mysql> create procedure sp_user_add(in in_username varchar(20),in in
(20))
    -> begin
    ->   insert into users(username,pwd)values(in_username,in_pwd);
    -> end $
Query OK, 0 rows affected (0.08 sec)

mysql>
```

2. Calling a stored procedure : sp_user_add

```java
import java.sql.*;
public class TestAdd {

    public static void main(String[] args) {
        DBUtil db = new DBUtil();
        Connection conn = db.openConnection();
        String sql = "call sp_user_add(?,?)";

        try {
            CallableStatement callStmt = conn.prepareCall(sql);
            callStmt.setString(1, "Solomen");
            callStmt.setString(2, "202020");
            callStmt.executeUpdate();
        } catch (SQLException e) {
            e.printStackTrace();
        } finally {
            db.DBClose();
        }
    }
}
```

Result:

JDBC Call Stored Procedure Update User

1. Create a stored procedure: sp_user_update in MySQL

```
DELIMITER $
create procedure sp_user_update(in in_id int,in in_username varchar(20),in in_pwd
varchar(20))
begin
  update users set username=in_username,pwd=in_pwd where id=in_id;
end $
```

2. Calling a stored procedure : sp_user_update

```java
import java.sql.*;
public class TestUpdate {

    public static void main(String[] args) {
        DBUtil db = new DBUtil();
        Connection conn = db.openConnection();
        String sql = "call sp_user_update(?,?,?)";

        try {
            CallableStatement callStmt = conn.prepareCall(sql);
            callStmt.setInt(1, 14);
            callStmt.setString(2, "Solomen");
            callStmt.setString(3, "303030");
            callStmt.executeUpdate();
        } catch (SQLException e) {
            e.printStackTrace();
        } finally {
            db.DBClose();
        }
    }
}
```

Result:

JDBC Call Stored Procedure Delete User

1. Create a stored procedure: sp_user_delete in MySQL

```
DELIMITER $
create procedure sp_user_delete(in in_id int)
begin
  delete from users where id=in_id;
end $
```

2. Calling a stored procedure : sp_user_delete

```java
import java.sql.*;
public class TestDelete {

    public static void main(String[] args) {
        DBUtil db = new DBUtil();
        Connection conn = db.openConnection();
        String sql = "call sp_user_delete(?)";

        try {
            CallableStatement callStmt = conn.prepareCall(sql);
            callStmt.setInt(1, 14);
            callStmt.executeUpdate();
        } catch (SQLException e) {
            e.printStackTrace();
        } finally {
            db.DBClose();
        }
    }
}
```

Result:

JDBC Call Stored Procedure Query User

1. Create a stored procedure: sp_user_find in MySQL

```
DELIMITER $
create procedure sp_user_find()
begin
  select * from users;
end $
```

2. Calling a stored procedure : sp_user_find

```java
import java.sql.*;
public class TestFind {

    public static void main(String[] args) {
        DBUtil db = new DBUtil();
        Connection conn = db.openConnection();
        String sql = "call sp_user_find()";

        try {
            CallableStatement callStmt = conn.prepareCall(sql);
            callStmt.executeUpdate();
            ResultSet rs = callStmt.getResultSet();
            while (rs.next()) {
                int id = rs.getInt("id");
                String username = rs.getString("username");
                String pwd = rs.getString("pwd");
                System.out.println(id + "," + username + "," + pwd);
            }
        } catch (SQLException e) {
            e.printStackTrace();
        }
    }
}
```

Result:

```
 Problems  @ Javadoc  Declaration  Console ☒          ▭  ☐

3,James,666666                                              ▲
4,Isacc,777777
6,David,111111
7,Sala,222222
8,Mathew,333333
9,Luka,4444444
10,John,555555
11,Ablahan,888888
12,Make,999999
13,Lebeka,101010
                                                           ▼
 ◄                                                    ►
```

JDBC Call Stored Procedure Return Parameter

1. Create a Add users and return the latest insert id: sp_user_add_id in MySQL

```
DELIMITER $
create procedure sp_user_add_id(in in_username varchar(20),in in_pwd varchar(20),out out_id int)
begin
  insert into users(username,pwd)values(in_username,in_pwd);
  select last_insert_id() into out_id;
end $
```

2. Calling a stored procedure : sp_user_add_id

```java
import java.sql.*;

public class TestAdd_Id {

    public static void main(String[] args) {

        DBUtil db = new DBUtil();
        Connection conn = db.openConnection();
        String sql = "call sp_user_add_id(?,?,?)";

        try {
            CallableStatement callStmt = conn.prepareCall(sql);
            callStmt.setString(1, "Sally");
            callStmt.setString(2, "404040");
            callStmt.registerOutParameter(3, Types.INTEGER);
            callStmt.executeUpdate();

            int id = callStmt.getInt("out_id");
            System.out.println("id : " + id);
        } catch (SQLException e) {
            e.printStackTrace();
        }
    }
}
```

Result: